THE HUMAN PATH ACROSS THE CONTINENTS

PATHWAYS THROUGH AFRICA

Heather C. Hudak

CRABTREE
PUBLISHING COMPANY
WWW.CRABTREEBOOKS.COM

CRABTREE
PUBLISHING COMPANY
WWW.CRABTREEBOOKS.COM

Author: Heather C. Hudak

Editorial director: Kathy Middleton

Editors: Rachel Cooke, Janine Deschenes

Design: Jeni Child

Photo research: FFP Consulting; Tammy McGarr

Proofreader: Melissa Boyce

Print and production coordinator: Katherine Berti

Produced for Crabtree Publishing Company by
FFP Consulting Limited

Images:
t=Top, b=Bottom, tl=Top Left, tr=Top Right, bl=Bottom Left, br=Bottom Right,
c=Center, lc=Left Center, rc=Right Center

Alamy
RZAF_Images: p. 12t; Joerg Boethling: p. 13bl; Kevpix: p. 13rc;
Nick Greaves: p. 14b; imageBROKER: p. 15t; Maciej Dakowicz: p. 17t;
Stephen Dorey ABIPP: p. 17b; Karin Duthie: p. 19t; Art Directors & TRIP:
p. 20t; Johnny Greig: p. 23t; Peter Treanor: p. 27l; Travelscape Images: p. 29b
Shutterstock
FOTOGRIN: title page; Shujaa_777: p. 4t; Thomas Wyness:
p. 5tr; africa924: p. 5bl; eFesenko: p. 8b; LMspencer: p. 9rc; Hailu Wudineh
TSEGAYE: p. 10b; Ungureanu Catalina Oana: p. 11b; Alexandra Tyukavina:
p. 15b; InnaFelker: p. 21t; Neil Bradfield: p. 21b; Tayvay: p. 22–23b; Jordi C:
p. 23b; Hailu Wudineh TSEGAYE: p. 24–25b; Roman Yanushevsky: p. 25t;
BOULENGER Xavier: p. 25b; Vladimir Zhoga: p. 26b; StreetVJ: p. 27t; Attila
JANDI: p. 29t
Ethio-Djibouti Railway: p. 11c

All other images from Shutterstock

Maps: Jeni Child

Library and Archives Canada Cataloguing in Publication

Title: Pathways through Africa / Heather C. Hudak.
Names: Hudak, Heather C., 1975- author.
Description: Series statement: The human path across the continents |
  Includes index.
Identifiers: Canadiana (print) 20190111992 | Canadiana (ebook) 2019011200X
  ISBN 9780778765998 (hardcover)
  ISBN 9780778766445 (softcover)
  ISBN 9781427123961 (HTML)
Subjects: LCSH: Human ecology—Africa—Juvenile literature. |
  LCSH: Africa—Juvenile literature.
Classification: LCC GF701 .H83 2019 | DDC j304.2096—dc23

Library of Congress Cataloging-in-Publication Data

Names: Hudak, Heather C., 1975- author.
Title: Pathways through Africa / Heather C. Hudak.
Other titles: The Human path across the continents.
Description: New York : Crabtree Publishing Company, 2019. |
  Series: The Human path across the continents | Includes index.
Identifiers: LCCN 2019023297 (print) | LCCN 2019023298 (ebook) |
  ISBN 9780778765998 (hardcover) |
  ISBN 9780778766445 (paperback) |
  ISBN 9781427123961 (ebook)
Subjects: LCSH: Human ecology--Africa--Juvenile literature. |
  Transportation--Africa--Juvenile literature. | Africa--Juvenile literature.
Classification: LCC GF701 .H83 2019 (print) | LCC GF701 (ebook) |
  DDC 304.2096--dc23
LC record available at https://lccn.loc.gov/2019023297
LC ebook record available at https://lccn.loc.gov/2019023298

Crabtree Publishing Company
www.crabtreebooks.com   1-800-387-7650

Printed in the U.S.A./082019/CG20190712

Published in Canada
Crabtree Publishing
616 Welland Ave.
St. Catharines, Ontario
L2M 5V6

Published in the United States
Crabtree Publishing
PMB 59051
350 Fifth Avenue, 59th Floor
New York, New York 10118

Published in the United Kingdom
Crabtree Publishing
Maritime House
Basin Road North, Hove
BN41 1WR

Published in Australia
Crabtree Publishing
Unit 3–5 Currumbin Court
Capalaba
QLD 4157

CONTENTS

AFRICA

The Human Path Across AFRICA

Welcome to Africa, the continent that is home to more than 1.2 billion of Earth's people. Africa is made up of 54 countries, one member state, and **10 territories**. Its vast landscapes are diverse, from lush rain forests to dry deserts. Africa's people are as diverse as its landscapes. They belong to thousands of **ethnic groups** and speak more than 2,000 different languages.

Maasai women
in Tanzania

▲ **THE MAASAI PEOPLE** of Kenya and Tanzania are one of the many ethnic groups that have thrived in Africa for thousands of years. They are **Indigenous** Africans, people who are native to the continent. Other Indigenous ethnic groups include the Berber, Fulani, Somali, and Zulu peoples.

Early Indigenous Africans, like the Maasai, developed **trade** routes that crisscrossed the continent. They used carts and pack animals, such as camels, to transport goods. Many people settled along the banks of major rivers, such as the Nile, Congo, and Zambezi. Access to water helped them live by farming and fishing. Others lived on the Mediterranean, Atlantic, and Indian Ocean coastlines. They used canoes and boats to travel and transport goods from one place to another.

▼ **EUROPEAN COLONISTS** arrived in Africa in the late 1800s and stayed until the mid-20th century. **Colonists** saw the continent as a land of opportunity and battled for control of it—and its peoples. Africa is known for its rich **natural resources**, such as oil, ivory, rubber, wood, diamonds, and **minerals**. Europeans built roads and railways to transport goods from mines in the center of the continent to seaside **ports**, to be sent to countries around the world. Small towns gradually grew into large cities that centered around **industries**.

Nineteenth-century diamond mine in South Africa

Traffic jam in Cairo, Egypt

▶ **AFRICAN CITIES** have grown incredibly quickly in the last 50 years. Today, four out of every 10 Africans live in **urban** areas. In cities, cars, buses, taxis, and trucks create massive traffic jams on overcrowded streets.

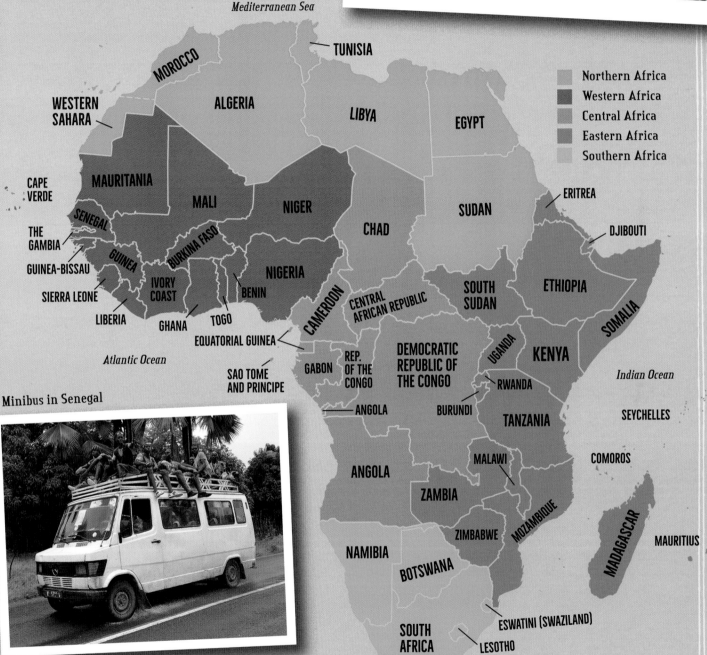
Minibus in Senegal

	Northern Africa
	Western Africa
	Central Africa
	Eastern Africa
	Southern Africa

Mediterranean Sea

MOROCCO
TUNISIA
WESTERN SAHARA
ALGERIA
LIBYA
EGYPT
CAPE VERDE
MAURITANIA
MALI
NIGER
ERITREA
SENEGAL
THE GAMBIA
SUDAN
DJIBOUTI
GUINEA-BISSAU
GUINEA
BURKINA FASO
CHAD
SIERRA LEONE
IVORY COAST
NIGERIA
BENIN
SOUTH SUDAN
ETHIOPIA
LIBERIA
GHANA
TOGO
CAMEROON
CENTRAL AFRICAN REPUBLIC
SOMALIA
EQUATORIAL GUINEA
Atlantic Ocean
SAO TOME AND PRINCIPE
GABON
REP. OF THE CONGO
DEMOCRATIC REPUBLIC OF THE CONGO
UGANDA
KENYA
Indian Ocean
ANGOLA
RWANDA
BURUNDI
TANZANIA
SEYCHELLES
MALAWI
COMOROS
ANGOLA
ZAMBIA
ZIMBABWE
MOZAMBIQUE
MADAGASCAR
MAURITIUS
NAMIBIA
BOTSWANA
ESWATINI (SWAZILAND)
SOUTH AFRICA
LESOTHO

▲ **IN RURAL COMMUNITIES** or desert regions, many people live in smaller villages and rely on farming. Vehicles are less common there. People often travel by foot or by riding animals across dusty trails and difficult **terrain**, or they squeeze into overcrowded buses. No matter the mode of transportation, a journey is a great way to discover a continent. This book explores the people and landscapes of Africa, through a variety of different journeys.

By Camel Through the SAHARA

Traders lead camels through the Sahara

The Sahara is one of the largest deserts on Earth. It covers most of North Africa. Travel across the vast, sandy dunes is a challenge. Camels are the only pack animals that can withstand the harsh desert for days at a time and still have the energy to carry people and cargo. For this reason, they are nicknamed ships of the desert. Traders have relied on camels to transport them through the desert for thousands of years.

⬆ **CAMEL CARAVANS,** or large groups of camels, have been used by traders since the third century. Thousands of animals transported salt, gold, dates, and other goods between towns, such as Marrakech and Fes in Morocco, and coastal ports. Others trekked right across the desert from Timbuktu in Mali to Cairo in Egypt. Today, modern four-wheel-drive vehicles have replaced large camel caravans. But many desert dwellers still use camels for travel, and for carrying goods across difficult terrain where vehicles cannot go.

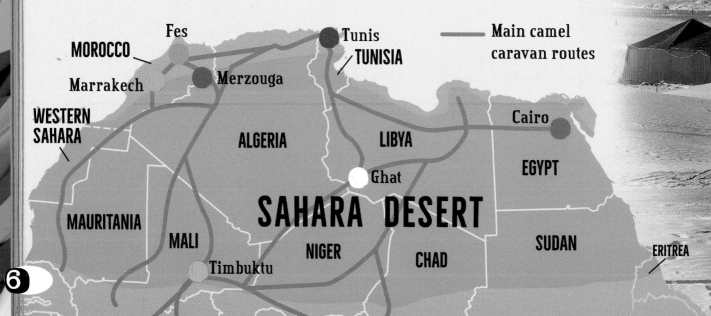

— Main camel caravan routes

Fes
MOROCCO
Marrakech
Merzouga
Tunis
TUNISIA
WESTERN SAHARA
ALGERIA
LIBYA
Cairo
EGYPT
Ghat
SAHARA DESERT
MAURITANIA
MALI
NIGER
CHAD
SUDAN
ERITREA
Timbuktu

Tourists riding camels near Merzouga

▶ **CAMEL RIDES** through the desert are very popular with tourists. They bring much-needed **income** into the **economy**. Merzouga, in Morocco, is a popular destination for camel treks. The small town is located just a few miles from the Erg Chebbi, the largest and highest sand dunes in the Sahara. Most tourists take a one-hour camel ride across the dunes to watch the spectacular sunset.

⬇ **THE PEOPLE OF THE SAHARA** mainly live in urban centers on the edge of the desert where there are reliable sources of food and water. Others live as nomads in the heart of the desert. They migrate often in search of **oases**, and raise sheep, goats, and camels that graze the land. They live in tents that are easy to move when there are no plants left for their herds to eat. Some nomads are traveling merchants. They sell their goods, including salt and fuel, from town to town.

The Sahara is one of the world's harshest environments. Extreme heat, strong winds, and lack of rainfall make it difficult for plants, animals, and people to survive. Only about 2.5 million people live there, despite the Sahara's huge area. Large parts of the desert have no people at all.

Nomad camp near Merzouga in the Sahara

PEOPLE ALONG THE WAY

Ibrahim was born in the desert and owns his own camel trekking company in Merzouga. He has learned many languages to enable him to guide visitors through the desert and to share his love and knowledge of the Sahara with them. At night, around the campfire, he plays music and tells riddles and jokes. It is important to him that he extends the Moroccan tradition of warm hospitality to his guests.

Sail Down the NILE RIVER

The Nile is the longest river in the world. It is a major transportation route and a vital source of water. Located in northeast Africa, the river snakes its way through 11 countries, including Egypt. Egypt was where one of the world's oldest civilizations took shape about 5,000 years ago. In ancient times, sailing along the Nile was the fastest and easiest way to travel. Boat travel remains a common mode of transportation on the river today.

▼ **LARGE CITIES ON THE NILE,** such as Cairo, Alexandria, and Luxor, are where most people in Egypt live. Much of the country's land is a barren desert, and there is next to no rain. The Nile provides a life-giving source of water. Each summer, the river floods, leaving behind thick, rich soil that is perfect for farming. Ancient Egyptians developed complex **irrigation** systems using water from the Nile to grow crops of wheat, flax, and papyrus. Over time, large cities rose up along the banks of the river. Today there are 100 million people in Egypt.

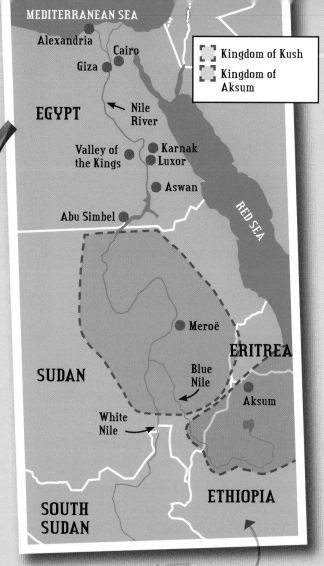

MEDITERRANEAN SEA

Alexandria
Cairo
Giza

EGYPT
Nile River

Valley of the Kings
Karnak
Luxor

Aswan

RED SEA

Abu Simbel

☐ Kingdom of Kush
☐ Kingdom of Aksum

Meroë

ERITREA

Blue Nile

Aksum

SUDAN

White Nile

ETHIOPIA

SOUTH SUDAN

EGYPT

City of Cairo and the Nile River

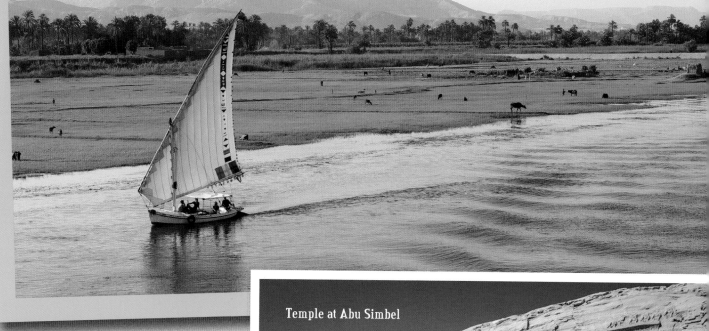

Temple at Abu Simbel

⬆ **FELUCCAS** are traditional wooden sailboats. Powered only by wind, they have been a main method of transportation on the Nile for centuries. Today, they are often used to transport tourists to Egypt's historic sites along the Nile.

Ancient Egyptians built elaborate tombs and temples on the banks between Aswan and Luxor. They believed the Nile River was the route between life and death. Most tourists board their feluccas in Aswan and sail toward Luxor. The boats stop at many points of interest, such as Luxor Temple and the Valley of the Kings.

In surrounding countries, the Nile extends to sites of other ancient civilizations that also used the river. Examples include the Kingdom of Kush and the Kingdom of Aksum.

⬆ **TOURISTS FLY TO ABU SIMBEL** from Aswan to see the rock temples there. Tourism is a major industry in Egypt. It is one of the nation's main sources of income and it creates many jobs. The country is home to some of the world's most famous ancient monuments, such as the Great Pyramids at Giza. But the large number of tourists has damaged these monuments, and work is underway to protect them.

Pause for REFLECTION

- Why do most people in Egypt continue to settle along the Nile?
- Why is a felucca an effective way to travel down the Nile?
- What effects does tourism have on Egypt and the Nile River?

SUDAN

ERITREA

Railway

ETHIOPIA

DJIBOUTI

Djibouti

Dewele

Addis
Ababa

Dire
Dawa

Adama

ETHIOPIA

SOMALIA

SOUTH
SUDAN

KENYA

Across
ETHIOPIA
by Rail

Addis Ababa is the capital of
Ethiopia and its main economic
center. A railroad links Addis
Ababa to the port city of Djibouti
in the Republic of Djibouti on
the northeast coast of Africa. This
connection is very important, since
Ethiopia is **landlocked**, and does not have
a port. The new rail line carries 70 percent
of all freight that passes through Djibouti. Like
all new modern railways, the line is electric,
which means it causes less air pollution.

⬇ **ADDIS ABABA,** the start of our journey, is one of the most
beautiful cities in Africa. The city is set on a lush **plateau** at
the foot of Mount Entoto in the center of Ethiopia. Nearly 3.4
million people live there, making it the largest city in Ethiopia.
Many international organizations have their main offices in
Addis Ababa, including the African Union and the United Nations
Economic Commission for Africa. These two organizations help
make important economic and political decisions for much of
Africa. Nearly all products sent to and from Ethiopia have to pass
through Addis Ababa on their way to port cities such as Djibouti.

African Union
building in
Addis Ababa

A RAIL LINE BETWEEN ETHIOPIA AND DJIBOUTI was first built in the early 1900s. It was not well maintained. By 2009, the railway was abandoned. People had to use roads to carry cargo to and from ports. But passage on the long, dusty roads was slow. It took three to four days to make the journey. In 2016, a new electric rail link was opened beside the old rail line. The new railroad cuts travel time down to just 10 hours. As a result, people can ship their goods to the ports much faster.

Yusuf Abera often makes the trip on the Ethiopia-Djibouti railway. He is a trader who lives in Addis Ababa, and he travels to inspect goods at Djibouti's port. Yusef much prefers the new rail service over the old one. He is happy that the journey is safer and more comfortable. He also pays only $25, while flights cost about $130.

Electric train on the new Ethiopia railroad

THE PORT OF DJIBOUTI is the final destination after a 470-mile (756 km) journey from Addis Ababa. From there, goods are **exported** to countries around the world. The new rail link has started a wave of **industrialization** across the farming nation. For example, new clothing and shoe factories have been built. As a result, Ethiopia's economy is now one of the fastest-growing in Africa. There are plans to extend the rail line to other parts of Ethiopia. This would make it easier to transport other items, such as coffee from western Ethiopia, to the port. In the future, the railroad could stretch all the way across Africa to the Atlantic Ocean.

Cranes loading goods at Djibouti's port

Trucking Flowers in KENYA

Truck on the highway to Nairobi

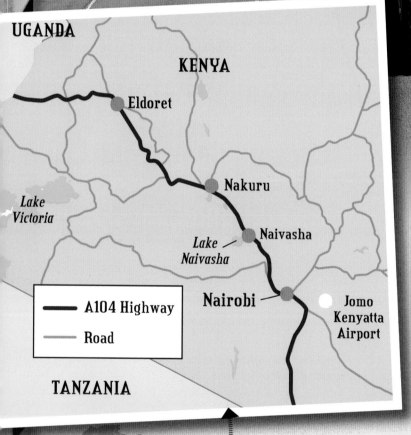

UGANDA

KENYA

Eldoret

Nakuru

Lake Victoria

Lake Naivasha

Naivasha

Nairobi

Jomo Kenyatta Airport

— A104 Highway

— Road

TANZANIA

KENYA

Agriculture is the biggest industry in Kenya. The country is home to about 50 million people, and 75 percent earn all or part of their living from agriculture. The warm, sunny climate is ideal for growing vegetables, coffee, tea, tobacco, cotton, fruits, and flowers. Each week, 3,000 tons (2,720 metric tons) of flowers are packed into boxes. They are loaded into refrigerated trucks headed for Nairobi, the capital of Kenya.

▶ **FLOWER FARMS** around Lake Naivasha produce more than 50 percent of Kenya's flowers. Flower farmers were drawn to the region in the late 1980s, thanks to the plentiful freshwater supply and the fact that it is very close to Nairobi. Today, more than 30,000 people work in the local flower industry. Across the country, about 90,000 people work on flower farms and more than 400,000 depend on the flower industry in some way.

◄···· **THE TRUCK DRIVE** from Lake Naivasha to Nairobi takes about two hours on the A104 highway. This major road provides easy access to Nairobi and the airport. It is also a transportation link to other major Kenyan cities, such as Nakuru and Eldoret. Nairobi is a transportation hub where flowers can be shipped by air to other parts of the world. The flower industry has helped Nairobi to grow in size.

Kenya has the largest economy in East Africa, but it is still a **developing nation**. Many people live in **poverty**. The growing demand for flowers and other farm products creates jobs in poor, **rural** areas. But the flower industry has also caused pollution in Lake Naivasha. Fertilizers used to feed the flowers poison the water, and fish and birds are dying. Because the population of the area is growing quickly, too much water is being taken out of the lake to be used in homes.

Pauline works at a flower farm by Lake Naivasha. Every morning, she is among the many women who leave their children at a daycare center near the farm. She works more than eight hours per day. Despite her long hours, Pauline lives paycheck to paycheck. The cost of rent in the area has skyrocketed, even when a family shares one room. Many workers struggle to support themselves and their families.

Flower workers in Kenya

Cargo at Nairobi's airport

▲ **NAIROBI'S JOMO KENYATTA AIRPORT** is well connected to major cities around the world. The airport even has a special terminal just for sorting, cooling, and transporting flowers quickly so they remain fresh. Every major airline that flies through Nairobi has space set aside for cut-flower cargo. Planes fly the flowers to Europe, Asia, the Middle East, Australia, and the Americas.

Barge Along the CONGO RIVER

CAMEROON

CENTRAL AFRICAN REPUBLIC

SOUTH SUDAN

Lisala Bumba

Kisangani

GABON

REP. OF THE CONGO

Congo River

Ubundu

RWANDA

BURUNDI

Brazzaville

DEMOCRATIC REPUBLIC OF THE CONGO

Kinshasa

Muanda

South Atlantic Ocean

ANGOLA

ZAMBIA

The Democratic Republic of the Congo (DRC) is one of the poorest countries in Africa. Most of its roads are in terrible shape. Often they are not safe to travel, so people travel by boat on the Congo River instead. For people who live in rural areas, the main river, and smaller ones that branch from it, are the only way to reach the big cities.

▼ **THICK RAIN FOREST** and rugged terrain make it hard to build roads in many parts of the DRC. Where there are roads, they have often been badly damaged in wars. More than half of the country's people live in small villages scattered across rural areas. They have adapted to live off the natural resources in their region. For instance, people who live in the forests hunt and fish, while those who live in the grasslands farm the land. But no matter where people live, transportation is not easy, and it is hard to bring in supplies.

Poor road through the rain forest, DRC

Timber barge on the Congo River

⬆ A POPULAR BARGE ROUTE travels between Kisangani, a large port city in northeastern DRC, and Kinshasa, the capital city. The most common boats are made up of a tug pushing one or two barges. Barges are flat boats meant to carry cargo only, but hundreds of people often squeeze onto them. Sometimes, the boats break down, get stuck in **silt** or mud, or become too full and capsize. Each barge is a floating market that is important to the local economy. People who live along the riverbanks paddle up to the barges in wooden canoes to buy and sell goods with the people on board. Barges transport beans, smoked fish, timber, palm oil, cassava flour, and charcoal from small towns to Kinshasa. On the return trip, they bring back **imported** materials, household goods, used vehicles, secondhand clothing, and canned foods.

⬇ KINSHASA has a population of more than 9 million people. It is the largest city in Central Africa and home to many businesses. People travel to the city hoping to find work there. But like most cities in the DRC, Kinshasa cannot provide proper housing, water, and sewage services to everyone living there.

Crossing the road in Kinshasa

Pause for REFLECTION

- Why is the Congo River so important to the people of the DRC?
- How do barges help the local economy of small towns and villages?
- How would better roads help people in the DRC?

15

Walking for Water in MALAWI

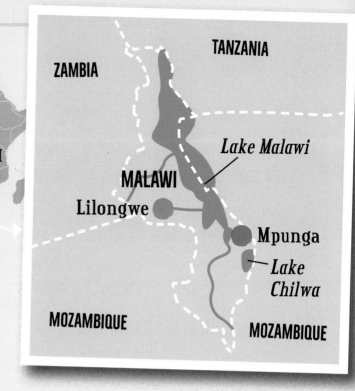

MALAWI

For many people in Africa, the lack of access to clean, safe water is a major challenge. There is water scarcity in many areas. Unclean water in other areas causes poor health and contributes to poverty. Each day, millions of women and children walk to and from rural villages to collect water. This is the situation for many people in Malawi, one of the smallest and least-developed countries in Africa.

⬇ **LAKE MALAWI,** a massive freshwater lake, covers much of the country, but the water in it is not safe to drink. Many other water sources are contaminated. About 19 million people live in Malawi, and one in three people do not have access to clean water. Deforestation and the overuse of farmland has led to flooding and soil **erosion**, which pollutes water sources like Lake Malawi. As a result of dirty water and poor sanitation, more than 3,100 children die from diseases or waterborne **parasites** each year.

Lake Malawi

PEOPLE
ALONG THE WAY

Ndogolo, the head of the village of Mpunga in Malawi, welcomes the improved water sanitation in his village. A community project, helped by an international charity, has given preschool children there more daycare and better toilets. It has taught them the best way to wash their hands. Mothers can work while their children are in daycare, and children are healthier.

Girls collecting water

↑ MALAWIANS OFTEN WALK to collect clean water from taps or pumps. Usually, this is a job for women and girls. The walks can take 30 minutes or more each day, with some women and girls beginning as early as 4 a.m. Some must make the journey more than once a day. Many develop arthritis and other conditions from walking so much while carrying a huge jug of water. Because of the time it takes to collect water, girls often miss school or are forced to drop out. Women are unable to work in other jobs.

↓ VILLAGE WATER PUMPS are key to solving these problems. The Malawi government, with the help of international aid, has spent millions building water systems in many communities. This has greatly improved access to clean drinking water. The government is also trying to improve sanitation, with access to decent toilets. However, water systems are hard to maintain. The growing population also puts pressure on the supply of water.

A new village water pump in use

Bush Plane Over BOTSWANA

Flying over the Okavango Delta

Botswana is one of the most popular safari destinations in Africa. Across the continent, tourism creates much-needed jobs for millions of people and is a strong source of income for many countries. In Botswana, tourists pay top dollar for a chance to explore the breathtaking Okavango Delta. One of the few ways to get to the **delta** is in a bush plane.

BOTSWANA

↑ MAUN is a tiny town on the Thamalakane River in northern Botswana. It is the starting point for many safaris. From there, bush planes carry people to lodges in the Okavango Delta that can only be reached by aircraft. More than 80 planes fly through Maun each day.

The Okavango Delta is one of the world's most unique ecosystems. From June to August, floods draw a wide variety of wildlife to the area. Traditionally, local peoples lived off the land as fishers, hunters, and gatherers. But then cattle farms and illegal hunting began to threaten their land and its wildlife. So the Indigenous Batawana people built the Moremi Game **Reserve**. It was the first reserve in Africa created by local residents. Today, nearly 45 percent of northern Botswana's people use their skills to conserve wildlife and nature in their communities.

Okavango Delta

ZIMBABWE

Moremi

Chobe National Park

Maun

NAMIBIA

BOTSWANA

Kalahari Desert

══ Plane journey
○ Safari lodges

Gaborone

Inside a diamond mine

◀ **DIAMOND MINING** has made Botswana one of the richest countries in Africa. Earnings from mining have helped pay for infrastructure. For instance, most city dwellers have access to safe, clean drinking water, and proper sanitation and sewage systems. Mining brings in more money than any other industry, but it also damages the environment. Water supplies are polluted, and soil is eroded. On the other hand, **ecotourism** can help protect nature, and give people a source of income. About 17 percent of Botswana's land is set aside for wilderness protection and wildlife **conservation** zones.

▼ **THE KALAHARI DESERT** to the south covers about two-thirds of Botswana. The dry, hot climate means the land is not suitable for growing large crops. People grow only the food they need for their families to live on. Many people rely on money from a family member who works in one of the country's urban centers or overseas. Nearly half of Botswana's 2.3 million people live in or within 62 miles (100 km) of Gaborone, the nation's capital.

PEOPLE ALONG THE WAY

Ben Jordaan is a bush pilot in Botswana. He lives in Maun, and he flies tourists in small planes over the Okavango Delta and the Kalahari Desert. Ben is always amazed by how the summer rains change the brown, dry landscape to an incredibly green and lush woodland. At this time of year, vast numbers of wild animals are on the move, including gemsbok (a type of antelope), wildebeests, and giraffes.

Gemsbok in the Kalahari Desert

BOTSWANA

MOZAMBIQUE

Pretoria

NAMIBIA

Kimberley

ESWATINI (SWAZILAND)

SOUTH AFRICA

LESOTHO

Cape Town

Beaufort West

Worcester

SOUTH AFRICA'S Famous Blue Train

South Africa is known for its stunning scenery, including mountains, plains, vineyards, forests, deserts, and beaches. One of the best ways to take it all in is a ride on the Blue Train, one of the most famous train lines in Africa. It links one side of the country to the other, from Pretoria in the northeast to Cape Town in the southwest.

▶ **THE BIG HOLE,** at Kimberley, South Africa, is an old **shaft** from one of the world's largest diamond mines. The Blue Train stops here, eight hours into the 30-hour trip. Kimberley was where the industrialization of South Africa began, when diamonds were discovered there in the mid-1800s. This boosted the economy and sparked a wave of settlers. Trains were used to bring people from the coast to the mines in the interior of South Africa.

Today, nearly 500,000 people work in the mining industry. South Africa produces more gold, platinum, and chromium than any other place in the world. It is also one of the top diamond producers. Because of the infrastructure built in the mineral-rich eastern part of the country, more than 90 percent of the nation's 57 million people live in this part of South Africa.

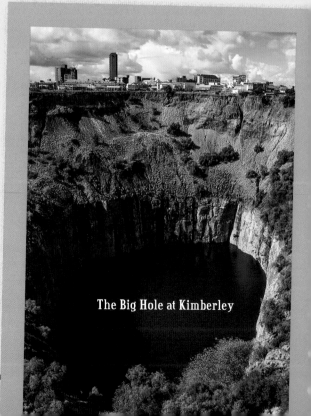

The Big Hole at Kimberley

Harbor at Cape Town

CAPE TOWN, our train's final stop, is the second-largest city in South Africa. Cape Town is often called the Mother City, since it was the site of the first European settlement in South Africa. Dutch settlers were the first to arrive. They were attracted to the area by the freshwater streams of Table Mountain that could be used as sources of clean drinking water.

SETTLERS brought enslaved people and laborers from places such as Madagascar, Guinea, India, and the Philippines to help develop the city. By the time slavery was abolished, Cape Town had become a diverse mix of ethnicities and races. Today, that diversity is still present in the many languages people speak, foods they eat, and music they make. However, Cape Town's population growth to more than 4 million has put pressure on water supplies. Shortages now occur regularly, in years when rainfall is low.

A street festival in Cape Town

Pause for
REFLECTION

- Why did people want to settle in South Africa?
- What role did trains play in the development of South Africa's mining towns?
- What makes Cape Town so diverse?

Rickshaw Ride in NIGERIA

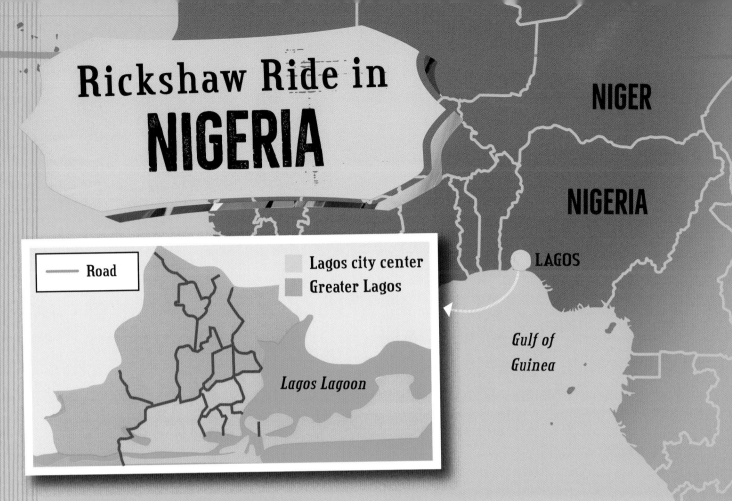

NIGER

NIGERIA

LAGOS

Gulf of Guinea

— Road

Lagos city center

Greater Lagos

Lagos Lagoon

Nearly 200 million people live in Nigeria. That is more people than any other country in Africa. About half of all Nigerians live in cities, such as Lagos. This city is the country's main commercial and financial center. With a population of about 21 million, Lagos is one of the fastest-growing cities in the world. The city is struggling to manage its growth.

Lagos is a major port city.

▶ **TRAFFIC IN LAGOS** is a huge problem. Each day, many **commuters** spend several hours traveling. The roads were not built to support the huge amount of traffic on them each day. If any of the major roadways become jammed, traffic across the entire city comes to a halt. A journey that sometimes can be done in 40 minutes may take as long as four hours.

Street sellers at work

Pause for

REFLECTION

- Why is Lagos growing so quickly?
- How would the people of Lagos benefit from better public transportation?
- Why are keke rickshaws so popular?

⬆ **A STREET CULTURE** has built up around Lagos' traffic problems. Many roads are used as a marketplace. People walk from one vehicle to the next, or hop from bus to bus, selling goods. Some drivers even sell goods from their vehicles. Many people only sleep a few hours each night. They get home late at night, and have to be on the road very early the next day to get to work on time.

↓ **KEKE NAPEP** are a fast way for people to get around Lagos. These motorized tricycles, or rickshaws, speed through the streets, going where four-wheeled cars cannot. They are often used for traveling short distances or on routes where buses do not stop. Drivers can take shortcuts to get to their destination faster. But keke rickshaws do not solve the traffic problems in Lagos. The government has a plan to help meet the needs of the growing city. There are many new bus routes across the city. New rail links will be built between busy business districts and the city's largest neighborhoods. Improved walking and cycling routes, ferry boats, and better roadways are also coming in the future.

Keke Napep rickshaw

Shipping Out of IVORY COAST

Major shipping routes

Genoa
Valencia
Algeciras
Dakar
IVORY COAST
ABIDJAN
Luanda
Durban
Cape Town
Colombo

More than 90 percent of Africa's imports and exports are transported by sea on ships. The Port of Abidjan is the largest port in West Africa and the second-largest on the entire continent. Located in Ivory Coast, millions of tons of cargo pass through the port each year.

▼ THE PORT OF ABIDJAN plays an important role in getting crop exports from rural farming areas to other parts of the world. Fuel, machinery, and food are also imported through the port. In fact, most of Ivory Coast's trade passes through Abidjan. The port also serves landlocked countries nearby, such as Mali, Burkina Faso, and Niger. It is well connected by highways, as well as the Abidjan-Niger Railroad, and an international airport. Ivory Coast earns about 60 percent of its income from traffic through the port.

The port is built along Ébrié **Lagoon**, which is cut off from the Atlantic Ocean by a narrow strip of land. The deep Vridi Canal connects the lagoon to the ocean, making it possible for large cargo ships to reach the port. More than half of all industries in Ivory Coast are found near the lagoon. The lagoon was once considered a symbol of beauty. Today, it is used as a garbage dump. The water is highly polluted with waste and sewage.

Cargo ships in the Port of Abidjan

City of Abidjan

Tianjin

Shanghai

Hong Kong

Singapore

⬆ **THE CITY OF ABIDJAN** has grown to be the financial, commercial, and industrial center of Ivory Coast, thanks to its coastal location and busy port. The modern city is known for its lush green spaces, as well as its museums, libraries, universities, and research institutes. Nearby tourist attractions, such as the tropical rain forest, bring in visitors.

⬇ **IVORY COAST** is home to more than 24 million people. About two-thirds of the population rely on the agriculture industry. Yams, cassava, plantains, rice, and corn are some of the main crops grown there. Many of these crops are used to feed local people. Coffee, timber, bananas, pineapples, and rubber are some of the biggest export crops. But cocoa beans are the most important. No country in the world produces more cocoa beans than Ivory Coast. More than 25 percent of the population grow cocoa bean crops.

Sorting cocoa beans

Pause for
REFLECTION

- How does the Port of Abidjan support the agriculture industry?
- What impact does the port have on the environment?
- Can you think of any ways that people can help lessen their impact on the environment in port cities?

25

MALI

NIGER

Dakar

SENEGAL

Bamako

Niamey

Ouagadougou

N'Djamena

BURKINA
FASO

NIGERIA

CHAD

CAMEROON

City of Dakar, Senegal

Drive the
TRANS-
AFRICAN
Highway

The African continent is developing quickly, but many people live in poverty. Trade between countries can help create more income. A strong transportation system is needed to move people and goods from one country to another. That is why the United Nations started the Trans-African Highway (TAH) project in the 1970s. The TAH helps connect countries so they can build stronger systems of trade.

Truck in Senegal

▲ **DAKAR** is a port city on the Atlantic Ocean. It is the capital of Senegal. Here we start our journey on the West African portion of the Trans-African Highway. This part of the highway passes through Mali, Burkina Faso, Niger, Nigeria, and Cameroon along the way to N'Djamena, a port city on the Chari River in Chad. This is the only completed section of the TAH so far. It forms a link between five capital cities and many towns and villages. Smaller roads that feed into the highway connect more **remote** regions and landlocked countries in West Africa to the ports along the coast.

ROADS are the main mode of transportation across Africa, but many are in poor shape. They are often made of dirt, and are difficult to travel on. Some even get washed out during heavy rains and floods. There is a lack of money to pave and care for roads. Drivers often come across roadblocks as they travel, with limited or no alternate routes. All of these factors cause major delays for travelers.

Stuck in the mud in Cameroon

Road under construction

BUILDING the Trans-African Highway helps solve the problems of poor roads, but construction has been very slow. About a fifth of the highway has not yet been built, and portions are still unpaved. Some countries lack the money they need to build roads. Others find it difficult to work with neighboring countries. In some places, the road is falling apart due to low construction standards, lack of care, and climate changes.

There is proof the Trans-African Highway is helping local people. For example, the number of trucks that travel daily from Kaya to Dori, in Burkina Faso, has nearly doubled. This is due to increased trade between Niger and Burkina Faso. Bus services from Kéniéba to Bamako, in Mali, have risen from once a week to 20 times a day. Today, the trip takes only about five hours. It took 28 hours before the road was built.

Pause for REFLECTION

- How do better roads help increase trade and reduce poverty?
- Why is the TAH less of a priority in some African countries?
- What factors prevent the TAH from being completed and maintained?

Bush Taxi Around
MAURITANIA

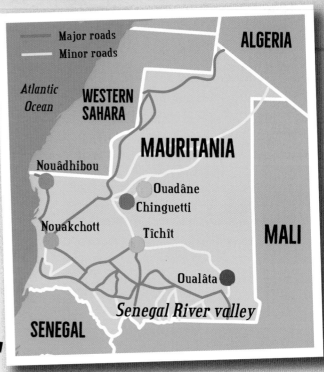

Major roads
Minor roads

Atlantic Ocean

WESTERN SAHARA

ALGERIA

MAURITANIA

Nouâdhibou

Ouadâne
Chinguetti

Nouakchott

Tîchît

MALI

Oualâta

Senegal River valley

SENEGAL

Mauritania is one of the least-developed and poorest nations in Africa. Most roads are in bad condition, and only one-third are paved. Some can be used for only part of the year due to shifting sand dunes and flooding, making it very difficult to get around. Bush taxis provide an important connection between communities.

MAURITANIA

⬇ **THE SAHARA DESERT** covers about three-quarters of Mauritania's land. It is very hot and dry, and sandstorms take place often. The very few people who live in this vast desert are nomads. They move in search of food, water, and grazing land for their animals.

Many people live in the Senegal River valley in the southernmost part of Mauritania. This region gets enough rain each year to allow people to earn their income from farming or raising **livestock**. But over the past few decades, there have been severe **droughts**. Land that was once good for farming has become desert, due to a lack of rain. As a result, people are moving to coastal urban centers, like Nouakchott, to find work and a better life.

The Sahara, Mauritania

Market in Nouakchott

⬆ **NOUAKCHOTT** is the capital of Mauritania and the start of our bush taxi journey. Located on the Atlantic coast, it was a small fishing town with only a few thousand people until the mid-1960s. Today, the city is home to nearly 1 million people. That is about a quarter of Mauritania's total population.

We are taking a bush taxi to Nouâdhibou, 300 miles (480 km) away to the northwest through the desert. Rich fishing resources have brought people to Nouâdhibou, Mauritania's second-largest city. **Iron ore** mines also draw many people to towns in the northern part of the country. Tîchît, Chinguetti, and Ouadâne are ancient cities that once relied on caravan trade with West African countries and Morocco. Today, they are thriving mining communities.

⬇ **BUSH TAXIS,** which are four-wheel-drive vehicles, are the best way to travel long distances on desert trails. Bush taxis do not run on a schedule. Drivers wait until their car is full before leaving for the next destination. Passengers may wait for hours or even days. As many as 30 people might cram into a vehicle. Crashes with animals, such as goats and camels, happen frequently. This makes driving at night extra dangerous.

Bush taxi in Mauritania

PEOPLE ALONG THE WAY

Ahmed is a bush taxi driver in Mauritania. He fills up his pickup truck with passengers in the capital, Nouakchott, then drives to Chinguetti in the Sahara. The road is paved part of the way, but later becomes a track through the sand. Ahmed struggles to find enough money to repair his truck, which is more than 20 years old, so he packs in as many passengers as possible for each journey.

GLOSSARY

agriculture Activities to do with growing crops and raising livestock

colonists People who settle and take control of a new land or region on behalf of a government

commuter A person who regularly travels, usually some distance, to and from work and home

conservation The protection of animals, plants, and natural spaces

delta A D-shaped area of flat land, often marshy, where a river or rivers empty into a sea or ocean

developing nation A poorer country with a lower standard of living, whose economy is usually based around farming. It is often in the process of changing to a more industry-based economy.

droughts Long periods of time with little or no rain

economy The system by which goods and services are made, sold, bought, and used

ecotourism Vacation travel that aims not to have a bad effect on the environment of the places visited. It often takes place in protected natural areas.

erosion Gradual wearing away due to natural forces such as wind and water

ethnic groups Groups of people who share the same cultural background, or are descended from the same family roots. For example, an ethnic group may have a common language.

exported Goods sent to be sold in another country

imported Goods brought into a country to be sold

income The amount of money a person, group, or region makes

Indigenous Describes people who naturally exist or live in a place rather than arrived from elsewhere

industrialization When a place becomes focused on using machines and factories for producing goods

industries Groups of companies that produce goods and services

iron ore Rock from which iron, a metal, is extracted

irrigation A system that supplies water to crops to help them grow

lagoon A shallow body of water partly enclosed by strips of land or a coral reef

landlocked A country that has no border or port on a sea or ocean

livestock Animals that are kept or raised for profit

minerals A solid, nonliving substance found in nature, often taken out of the ground by mining

natural resources Useful or valuable materials and substances in nature, such as trees or gold

oases Small parts of the desert where water and plants are found

parasites Organisms, or living things, that live inside other living things, and may cause diseases

plateau An area of mainly flat, high ground

ports Places where ships load and unload cargo

poverty The state of not having enough money for basic needs, such as food, clothing, and shelter

remote Describes a place far from large settlements

reserve In Africa, an area of land set aside to protect wildlife, plants, and landscape

rural Having to do with the countryside

shaft A deep hole dug into the ground for the purpose of mining

silt Particles of sand, soil, and mud carried in a river and dropped by its waters elsewhere

terrain The ground, or a piece of land

territories Places owned or ruled by a government

trade Buying and selling goods and services

urban Having to do with cities or towns

Further INFORMATION

BOOKS

Duhig, Holly. *Cultural Contributions from Africa: Banjos, Coffee, and More.* PowerKids Press, 2018.

Lonely Planet Kids. *Not for Parents Africa: Everything You Ever Wanted to Know.* Lonely Planet Kids, 2013.

Rockett, Paul. *Mapping Africa.* Crabtree Publishing, 2017.

WEBSITES

www.ducksters.com/geography/africa.php
Check out facts and figures about Africa, with links to further information about its individual countries.

www.worldbank.org/en/region/afr
Learn about World Bank projects that help grow the economies of developing countries in Africa.

www.un.org/sustainabledevelopment/water-and-sanitation
Read about the UN Sustainable Development Goals, which aim to create a world in which no one is left behind. Goal 6 is to provide clean water and sanitation to all people.

INDEX

ABOUT THE AUTHOR

Heather C. Hudak has written hundreds of children's books. When she is not writing, Heather enjoys traveling the world, from the beaches of Brazil to the African savanna. She also loves camping in the mountains near her home with her husband and many rescue pets.